The **primary** guide to...

HEADSHIP

Geoff Southworth

pfp, London

© 1996 **pfp**

First published in Great Britain in 1996 by
pfp
61 Gray's Inn Road
London WC1X 8TL

Printed in the UK

All rights reserved. No paragraph of this publication may be reproduced, stored in a retrieval system, copied or transmitted without written permission from the Publisher.

The author asserts his moral right to be identified as the author of this work.

ISBN 1 874050 28 7

A catalogue record for this book is available from the British Library.

Contents

	Introduction	*iv*
1	What we know about primary headship	1
2	Key tasks of headship	8
3	Skills and qualities of heads	19
4	Leadership	25
5	Working with your deputy	37
6	Ways of influencing teaching	45
7	Working with others	54
8	Managing yourself	62
	Conclusion	68
	Further reading	71
	Index	72

Introduction

This book is written for recently and newly appointed primary headteachers in their first headship but it should also appeal to more experienced headteachers since it draws upon many ideas which should contribute to all heads' thinking and professional development. The book is also relevant to the work and concerns of deputy heads, especially those who are acting heads, plan to apply for headship or are already candidates for a headship and about to be interviewed.

This is not a how-to-do-headship type of book. Rather it aims to provide a set of ideas about primary school leadership and management drawn from recent research, current thinking and successful practices of new and experienced primary practitioners. The ideas presented here aim to encourage readers to reflect on their own perspectives and actions, to look critically at their own perceptions, assumptions and experiences of school leadership and to adopt and try out some of the ideas. This is a practical book but, like all effective practice, it is underpinned by theoretical knowledge.

For ease of reading, all references to teachers, children and parents in this book are female.

Chapter 1

What we know about primary headship

What is it like to be head of a primary school? Like most jobs, it's a combination of things, most notably excitement and frustration, challenge and reward. The excitement comes from being in such a responsible position. As head, you have a great deal of influence in the school. Indeed, your position gives you the potential to be more influential than any other individual connected with the school.

On some days, though, it won't feel as if you have much influence. There will be unexpected callers and urgent phone messages. Forms will need completing and signing. Staff might be absent and the computer might have crashed.

These are some of the challenges of headship – trying to ensure that the school runs smoothly as an organisation. The rewards come not so much from keeping the school running, as from improving the quality of the school. That's the real challenge of headship and, when it happens, the most satisfying part of the job.

Arising from this broad view of the job there are five statements we can make about the work. Let's look at each in turn.

1 Heads need to offer some leadership

From a number of studies into effective schools and school improvement, we know that heads make a difference to their schools. If you've worked in a school where there has been a change of head, you might have experienced how individual heads create different effects in the same school.

Heads themselves believe they make a difference – that's one of the attractions of the role. The influence that comes with the position enables them to make a contribution to the school and its development. As key players in their schools, heads need to be able to provide some leadership and offer a sense of purpose and direction. Research shows that heads who offer 'purposeful leadership'

- understand the needs of the school
- are actively involved in the work and life of the school
- involve other colleagues and stakeholders
- don't try to exert total control over the staff
- influence the quality of teaching in the school
- participate in curricular developments and decisions
- develop whole-school policies
- create with colleagues and governors a school development plan
- monitor pupils' progress
- know what is happening in the classrooms and around the school
- ensure there are plans and records of what is taught
- contribute to the development of staff.

These ideas will be dealt with in other chapters. Here they show how leaders do things. They think and talk and they also get on with tasks.

Chapter 1 **What we know about primary headship**

2 Heads need to manage the school as an organisation

Heads have to ensure that there are efficient and effective management structures and systems.

- Staff roles and duties need to be as clear as possible.
- Classes and teaching groups need to be organised.
- Arrangements for planning, recording and reporting on the curriculum and pupils need to be established and sustained.
- School policies need to be devised and implemented.
- The school office needs to work well in order to facilitate the flow of internal and external communications.
- Accounts and budget systems need to be organised.
- Equipment and site concerns – from paper supplies to leaking toilets – need to be attended to.

Rather than adding more and more to such a list of matters to be dealt with, consider the following points.

First, although, as head, you have to ensure these systems are in place, you don't need to do them all or, indeed, very many yourself. In fact, if you find yourself dealing with a lot of these issues, the system might need looking at. Your job is to make sure that there are structures for dealing with these things. If that structure turns out to be that you are doing it, it needs amendment.

Second, one of the things that distinguishes more effective schools from others is that in successful schools things work – the photocopier functions properly, documents are properly filed and retrieved, supplies are accessible and kept in good order, replacement equipment arrives in good time, classroom supplies and materials are accessible, freely available and meet the needs of curricular policies and schemes of work.

Third, part of good management is ensuring that staff aren't frustrated by poor materials, broken equipment or lack of organisation. When striving to eliminate negative feelings, look for the positive too. When things work, recognise and explicitly value them. In management take nothing for granted. Praise colleagues for their efforts and successes. In a smooth running organisation there is positive reinforcement in plenty.

3 Heads are school developers

Leadership and management are needed to enable the school to move forward and develop. On a day-to-day basis much of a head's time is taken up with management. However, to exercise leadership heads need to be working towards improving the quality of the teaching and learning in the school – often with contributions from the deputy, senior staff, coordinators and governors.

Schools should be well maintained and sometimes changes will be needed in the way the school is managed and organized. For example, you might want to improve communications with parents or to smarten up the school's brochure. But such developments shouldn't happen at the expense of efforts to improve what is happening in classrooms.

The fundamental thing is to resolve to sustain a strong focus on teaching and learning. Lots of other things will distract you from this goal, but research shows that concerted attention on pupils and their learning makes a significant contribution to the school's success.

The next thing to recognise is that the quest for improvements in quality is never ending. There is no point at which you can say that it's finished. Perfect schools don't exist. Even in effective schools there are areas which need to be developed.

Chapter 1 **What we know about primary headship**

Of course, there need to be times when you appreciate how far the school has improved and value the efforts everyone has made. But school improvement is an ongoing process.

Developing the school is a long haul. It is less like a sprint than a marathon. Heads need to invest much of their precious, hard pressed time into it. Without their involvement and support, the school won't improve. Moreover, others need to be involved. As well as staff participation in the process, you need to enlist the support of the school's governors. Parents need to be kept informed of initiatives. The children also might be made aware of planned changes.

4 Headship is hard work

By now you might be wondering why anyone would want to be a head. As stated at the start of this chapter, it's a demanding and challenging job. For all the reasons set out or implied in the previous three sections, headship is plainly hard work.

As a head, you're never short of things to do. There's always someone to phone or visit, something to read and something happening. Many heads enjoy the variety of the work and dealing with the unexpected.

It's also the case that days at work are long. Many heads are amongst the first to arrive and the last to leave the premises. Heads increasingly are back in school in the evenings for governor and sub-committee meetings, parent meetings and workshops, fund-raising events and school performances, such as concerts and plays. Headship is a day job with a night shift!

On top of this, there is the never-ending process of improving the school. At times this can feel less like an exciting journey and more like being on a treadmill. Especially when there are numerous frustrations to deal with, such as reluctant colleagues, interpersonal tensions, external demands for changes to be made and problems with the building or plant to overcome. These can all add to feelings of exasperation.

So the work is not only demanding but tiring, too. You need to be fit to be a head. You have to be aware of the pace you're working at and, sometimes, be prepared to change your pace. Slowing down can be important, particularly if you've been in hyperdrive for a spell. Exhausted heads aren't much good to anyone, including themselves.

5 Becoming a head takes time

Although new heads in their first appointment start to be head of the school on day one, it does take some time to become accustomed to the role. Initially, you have to take stock of the school and of what you need to do. At first it can feel not only different being a head, compared with what you were in your previous role, but also rather strange.

The strangeness isn't simply being unfamiliar with the school and the role. It's also about becoming accustomed to the amount of influence you can wield. At first, many new heads find the weight of responsibility rather daunting. Others experience a sense of loneliness and isolation. The realisation that the 'buck stops with me' can be overwhelming for a while.

What is happening here is that new heads are trying on the mantle of headship and experiencing how it fits. As part of coming to terms with the role, heads realise in a profound and personal way that they are accountable for the school in a way they probably never have been before. Suddenly, parents, staff and governors expect you to have answers and to know things.

Chapter 2 **What we know about primary headship**

Sometimes you do, sometimes you don't. Then the mantle of headship feels like the emperor's new clothes!

Taking on a new role takes time. You might need to find a mentor. Mentoring for new heads is now established in many parts of England and Wales. Should you wish to work with a partner head, mentoring offers a valuable way of adapting to the role.

There are two other options. First, make contact with other heads in the locality. Some have informal meetings or established support groups which you might want to join. Second, look into schemes such as the HEADLAMP programme. Contact the Teacher Training Agency (TTA) or ask your professional association for details..

These insights into headship show that heads need to be able to

- manage their time, including preserving some personal time
- prioritise tasks and actions
- process lots of information about the school
- develop staff and themselves
- form professional judgments about the quality of the teaching and learning, as well as the school as an organisation
- explain, defend and justify these judgments to colleagues and stakeholders
- determine actions to be taken and make plans
- recognise and value the strengths and successes in the school.

These skills are an outline sketch of the key tasks of headship and of the competences you need to be an effective headteacher. Chapter 2 looks in greater detail at these key tasks.

Chapter 2

Key tasks of headship

This chapter looks at the main ingredients of primary headship. What do you need to do? There are seven areas to be considered but, before focussing on them, there are two introductory points to make.

First, the tasks are described in broad terms in order to provide reasonable coverage of the full scope of school management activities. Many of these tasks will be shared with other colleagues. Also, quite how far individual heads are directly involved with these areas will depend on your own perceptions of

- the school's needs
- colleagues' strengths
- your own abilities
- the school's specific circumstances.

The seven areas to be considered are task areas which, as a school, you need to ensure are being dealt with. This doesn't mean you have to do them all yourself.

The second point follows from the first. In attending to these tasks, you need to think about how to involve others, how and to whom to delegate. Consider involving the school's governors, senior management colleagues and all other members of staff. Take account of others, including parents and the local community.

Chapter 2 **Key tasks of headship**

The second point in particular could be taken to mean that a massive consultation process needs to be established and sustained. Sometimes that might be the case. More realistically though, there are ways of avoiding cumbersome communication processes. There are several key individuals to involve and rely on.

- The deputy head (or assistant head as some now prefer) should be involved in any consideration of these tasks. It's part of a deputy's responsibility and professional development to assist the head in reviewing and developing these task areas.
- The chair of governors needs to be involved throughout. Her knowledge of the school and the governors' preferences is valuable intelligence. She can also play the role of 'sounding board' for ideas and options. Moreover, many of the decisions arising from the task areas below will need to be formally reported, discussed and agreed with the school's governors. Governors can't be ignored, so it's good management practice to involve them from an early point.

Parent governors can be invited and deployed to find out the views of parents or a sample of parents on some specific issue, for example, the teaching of reading or the school's homework policy. Such a strategy enables the parent governors to have a meaningful role and helps the school staff to understand how their work is being perceived.

- Clerical staff and other members of staff who live in the school's vicinity can be enlisted to provide information about the community. In the case of church schools, vicars and priests should be involved, as well as other appropriate religious and community leaders.

The important point to stress is that heads shouldn't always rely on their individual perspectives. We are all prisoners of our own perceptions. No-one has 20/20 vision when managing a complex, social organisation such as a school. To avoid the pitfalls of partial perceptions and personal prejudices, try to develop a multi-perspective view.

We can now look at the seven key task areas and briefly discuss each of them.

1 Determine the overall aims, objectives and ethos of the school

This task area is concerned with the educational, social and moral values the school aims to promote and teach. What do we want the children to learn? That is the basic question which underscores this area. Much of this is covered by the National Curriculum or Scottish guidelines in terms of content and knowledge. In addition, issues such as equal opportunities, individual rights and responsibilities, respect, honesty, dignity and behaviour need to be considered.

Moreover, the aims, objectives and ethos need to be monitored. All schools have statements of aims and these are usually fine sounding sentiments. But are they in place? Take a look around the playground on a windy lunchtime and listen to how the midday assistants speak to some of the children. Are the staff harassed and pressed? How sensitive are they to certain children's needs?

This kind of analysis leads to a consideration of the school's ethos. Ethos is a difficult word to define, but it refers to the overall quality of life and experience in the school. These aspects contribute to whether the children feel they are well looked after, cared for, listened to and valued. It's to do with

Chapter 2 **Key tasks of headship**

the values the school actually conveys to the children and to all other members of the school's community. It can be elusive to describe, but can knock you out when it's either very positive or very negative.

As head, it's one of your tasks to examine what the ethos really is. Not only do you need to express the values you and others want to promote, your actions must reflect these values. You must set the example.

Furthermore, you need to check whether others are doing likewise and determine whether the children can actually detect those values in their experience of the school. For example, do the children perceive their efforts as being valued?

Ethos is a slippery concept, but is something that needs to be investigated seriously and managed.

2 Make school policies and plans

There is a clear need during the first months of your headship to evaluate the school's work and to begin to formulate ideas about the next school development plan. In working towards the new plan, you will need to continue with and incorporate existing priorities. There should also be scope for some new ideas to be included. Framing the next school development plan will be a key task for you in making a contribution to the school's improvement.

At the same time, current policies will need to be reviewed to examine their relevance and the extent of their implementation. In the medium term, some might need to be revised and updated. A few might have to be changed.

Alongside this review of policies and plans, a careful audit of the school's financial position and budgetary plans is necessary. The existing budget plan should be examined and the prospects for the coming year anticipated. There might be scope for extra investment in some aspects of the school. New priorities in the next development plan could even be given a financial boost. Certainly, school improvement plans should be linked to the school's financial position and possibilities explored.

Other resources should also be examined, particularly staff resources. The arrival of a new head marks not only a change of leader, but also a new member of staff. The new head's curricular strengths and interests can make a difference to how other staff play a part in the school. This sense of difference is especially true in medium-sized and smaller primary schools. In a five-teacher school, for example, a change of head marks a 20 per cent change in the teaching staff. The new head might be able to provide curricular leadership in some specific areas and 'free up' those staff who are coordinating those areas to contribute to other areas.

In a sense, the new head needs to think strategically about where the school is and where it might be heading.

3 Monitor, evaluate, develop and implement curricular and quality improvements

An incoming head is well placed to take a cool and reasonably detached look at the school's present position. She can conduct an audit of the school's strengths and constraints and put forward proposals for development. But any proposals need to be based on actual evidence of what is and isn't happening in the school. The new head should try to monitor

Chapter 2 **Key tasks of headship**

how the school is functioning and what is taking place in classrooms. She should also involve others in this process.

Once the monitoring has yielded some information, this needs to be evaluated by the head, senior management team, teaching staff and, if appropriate, others. Ideas emerging from the evaluation discussions should be shared with the chair of governors. Evaluation of the evidence can raise suggestions for developments as well as recognition of what is sound and should be valued.

This monitoring and evaluation obviously relates to the planning cycles in the school as discussed above. Therefore, plans need to be formulated in the light of the review discussions. The plans will contain the developments and improvements sought in the school and in classrooms. Yet the process doesn't stop here.

The next thing is to devise implementation plans, so that the carefully formed and agreed goals are put into practice. Then the implementation of policies and plans needs to be monitored and the whole process repeated.

Chapter 1 stated that effective heads know what is going on in the school and in the classrooms. To recap a few of those points, heads

- understand the needs of the school
- are actively involved in the work and life of the school
- involve other colleagues and stakeholders
- influence the quality of teaching in the school
- participate in curricular developments and decisions
- develop whole-school policies.

Monitoring and evaluation are two of the ways heads can put these ideas into practice.

4 Manage personnel

Running a school is a collective task. One of the arts of management is maximising the potential of colleagues. There are libraries full of books dealing with personnel management issues, so in this small section all that can be offered are a few basic ideas.

The selection and appointment of staff is a vital process and one which needs to be planned and performed with care and skill. There should be existing policies which the governors' personnel sub-committee has to hand. You might want to revise these – depending on how you saw your own selection process. It's worth looking at them, even though it may be some time before you can appoint staff.

Induction procedures also need to be thought through. Selecting the best person is important, but so too is getting that person settled into the school. Induction of staff is as important as selecting them.

Staff appraisal schemes should be governed by guidelines already in the school. Staff need to be appraised so that their efforts and successes can be formally recognised and their contributions valued. Appraisal also allows each teacher's individual development needs to be considered and action plans formulated.

Most teacher and staff appraisal systems in schools follow a developmental model. The aim of such systems is to enhance the performance of individuals. However, there is also a place for review where the head lets her colleagues know where they stand. In other words, heads might need to consider putting in place review meetings with staff in which they clearly and constructively, with evidence and criteria, set out how the individual's work performance is perceived. These meetings

Chapter 2 **Key tasks of headship**

are essentially 'reviews' of an individual's work and are sometimes a necessary support to the appraisal process.

Appointment, induction and appraisal are three important parts of personnel management. So too is having policies for staff grievances, equal opportunities, pay and redundancy. More than ever before, heads are not only managing people, but in a legal and bureaucratic sense are personnel managers and need to be mindful of colleagues' rights and responsibilities. Staff will therefore need job descriptions and these should be revised from time to time.

The other area which needs to be highlighted here is that of staff development. Teacher development has already been introduced as a part of the appraisal process. Whilst this is a necessary aspect of development, it's not sufficient in itself. For a head to lead her school's improvement efforts, attention must be paid to developing the staff as individuals, teams and as a group. The school won't improve unless staff – teachers, classroom assistants and others – develop.

An audit of colleagues' strengths is useful – determining areas where they don't feel confident and aspects of their teaching and practice where they feel they would benefit from further help. Again, priorities need to be established to meet these needs. All of this has then to be aligned with the school's priorities and the INSET and staff development budget.

One further thought – staff need to develop not because they are weak or poor, but because they are educators. Educators are life-long learners, concerned with getting better and improving their abilities to serve the children. It's important, therefore, that heads also model this, participate in development events and take their own professional development and learning seriously.

5 Ensure efficient and effective administration and site management

Several aspects of this area have been discussed already, so not much more is needed. The school premises and the grounds should be cared for. The caretaker/cleaner-in-charge/school keeper will be an important figure here, as will her staff and agency. It's worth noting that they see the school from a different perspective, which should not be undervalued simply because it is different.

The same applies to school office staff. Some, in effect, will be the head's personal assistant. Others in name, or in responsibility, will be the school's bursar. Each has an important role to play in maintaining the efficiency of the school as an organisation.

Each of these individuals will also have a significant impact – positive or negative – on the head's work. Devote time to ensuring that you all work together in a structured and organised way. There needs to be a careful and sensitive negotiation of roles. But this process must take place within the framework of the headteacher being able to offer educational leadership to the school as well as managing the school's support systems.

School office staff all contribute to the school's efficiency and to the effectiveness of your educational leadership.

6 Promote community relations and supply information

It is a particular challenge of the role that heads need to balance both internal demands and tasks whilst remaining aware of external relations. Parents in particular need to be

Chapter 2 **Key tasks of headship**

kept informed of what goes on in the school and what is about to happen. There is much truth in the notion that informed parents are happy ones.

Heads need to promote positive relations and a positive image of the school. Every meeting with parents is an opportunity to promote the work of the school. Better still, every meeting with parents is an opportunity to inform of the progress that their children are making. Clearly, arrangements for reporting to parents are a major responsibility.

Involving parents in the work of the school is equally important. Classroom support, invitation speakers, after-school clubs and a host of other activities provide ways of involving parents. Similarly, there is scope for involving other members of the local community.

Schools need to reach out to parents and to the community. Heads need to lead this, but they also need to orchestrate it because other staff (eg. teachers of reception class children) might have an important role to play in the communication process.

Governors can also contribute to the information flow and play an active part in ensuring that others know what is going on. Reference has been made to parent governors. Co-opted governors and foundation governors may be significant members of the community and so might be encouraged to promote the school and to provide information about it.

There are many different ways in which schools can disseminate information and sustain healthy relations. The most important thing is that they try to do so and use a range of ways rather than just a small handful.

7 Be accountable

Throughout much of the discussion runs the message that schools are public utilities and accountable to their stakeholders. Heads should always be ready to

- explain what's happening in the school
- justify why the school operates as it does
- defend the educational, social and moral values the school promotes.

More than ever before, heads must set out for staff, parents, governors, inspectors and others what the school is doing and why.

All of these tasks have implications for the skills and qualities heads need to use and to develop to be effective school leaders. Chapter 3 looks at these.

Chapter 3
Skills and qualities of heads

This chapter focusses on the skills and qualities which research shows are associated with effective headteachers. However, before looking at what these are, it's worth saying that there are difficulties in setting them down.

For one thing, there's a tendency for readers to feel they constitute the job description of a saint. For another, such specifications not only suggest that effective heads are superhuman, but that by comparison, the reader is somewhat inadequate.

The intention here is not to make you feel bad about yourself. Rather, the aim of this chapter is to help you think about your own strengths and one or two areas you might want to develop or focus on during your day-to-day work.

The following ideas have been developed from the work of Bolam *et al* (1993), who investigated what heads, and especially teachers, had to say about effective school leaders. The items on the list are therefore the *followers'* views about successful heads. This makes the ideas all the more pertinent and powerful since these are the skills staff are apparently looking for in their leaders. They are presented here as a set of bullet point statements with which you might agree or disagree.

There are also more subtle ways of using this material. You might, for example, not only say you agree or disagree with the statements, but also try to determine why you think so.

Another option is to use the statements to develop a discussion with your deputy or assistant headteacher. You could also extend this discussion to members of the senior management team. One reason for using the list in this way is to consider whether these skills and qualities are offered by more than one leader and to check that at least someone in the school is paying attention to them and is providing them. The statements might, therefore, help you analyse the nature and distribution of leadership in your school. They might also enable you to identify some professional development opportunities for yourself and colleagues.

Effective leaders

Personal qualities

Effective leaders in schools

- try to be professional in their dealings with everyone – they are open and honest, firm but fair with staff and consistent as they respond to individuals' requests
- are committed to the pupils and put their concern for the children's well-being and education before personal advancement
- work hard and show commitment to the school
- are well-organised and well-prepared
- are approachable and accessible
- display enthusiasm and optimism – they have a positive outlook and try to be constructive rather than being negative and overly critical
- don't take advantage of their position and are prepared to help out around the school and take their turn.

Chapter 3 **Skills and qualities of heads**

Managerial qualities

Effective leaders in school

- have a vision for the future development of the school which is based upon a personal philosophy and educational values which they can articulate to others
- plan ahead and think in a strategic way about the development of the school
- consult with others, listening to their ideas and responses to proposed initiatives (following wide consultation, they determine the overall direction and strategy and involve staff in the implementation of what has been agreed)
- delegate responsibilities to colleagues, providing them with the necessary support to carry out these duties and expecting them to follow through their tasks and to be accountable for their efforts
- ensure that there are effective whole-school structures in place
- from time to time are forceful, but not dictatorial – they can drive things along, but also remain sensitive to staff feelings and circumstances, ie. they can maintain a balance between pressure and support
- accept that they are ultimately responsible for the school but don't use this as a lever for always getting their own way
- are decisive when the situation requires it, for example when consultation shows that there is no consensus on an issue they are willing to make a decision and set out a course of action
- try to secure the support of colleagues and their commitment to ideas, proposals and plans – striving at all times to develop a sense of trust between themselves and staff and working at building and sustaining a sense of community and a culture of working together

- keep staff and stakeholders informed, work hard at ensuring there is a healthy flow of communication and develop their capacity to listen to what others are saying and are concerned about
- act on information and the views of staff, so that consultation is seen to be genuine and not insincere or manipulative
- emphasise the central importance of quality in the school's operations and encourage colleagues to hold high expectations of themselves, the children and each other
- are aware of new initiatives – yet avoid 'jumping on bandwagons' – and by preparing colleagues for future developments they reduce the amount of *ad hoc* decision-making and crisis management in the school, yet they also avoid overwhelming colleagues with new priorities
- demonstrate, through their actions and speech, that they are in touch with everyday life in the school
- work hard to motivate staff by offering encouragement and active support and by acknowledging their endeavours and praising their successes
- convey to staff that they have their concerns and well-being at heart – by facilitating the development of staff, providing opportunities for them to play a leadership role and listening to their concerns, plans and ambitions
- protect staff from political disputes and back them publicly in disputes involving external agencies.

On the first reading, this list can seem to be a daunting set of skills and qualities. But let's just reflect on this for a moment. When you look through them again, ask yourself the question, how many of these apply to what effective teachers do in their classrooms and around the school? Almost all of these apply to effective teachers.

Chapter 3 **Skills and qualities of heads**

Therefore, what you are faced with is not a huge personal development programme because you do not possess these skills and qualities. Rather, the issue is how do you now utilise these skills when working across the whole school and with many more adults than you might have formerly been used to dealing with.

There are three other points to add. First, this list is an amplification of the items set out on page 2. Indeed, there are strong links between this list and what's said in Chapters 1 and 2. These qualities are grounded in what's now known about effective schools, effective leadership and successful headteachers.

Second, the job is clearly a complex one. However, it's not a job you have to do by yourself. Although you're personally responsible for ensuring that the school runs smoothly and is developing the quality of the education provided for the children, you don't have to do this all by yourself. By definition, a school is a corporate organisation – it's made up of other members of staff. The art of headship is helping them to play their part.

Third, there are some statements here which sound contradictory. For example, on the one hand you are urged to be consultative and considerate, on the other you are encouraged to be firm and decisive. This apparent inconsistency is in fact a recognition of the need for leaders to try to balance competing needs. Colleagues like to be involved and to have a voice. But they don't want to sit in seemingly endless meetings waiting for someone to make up their mind. The key word here is balance. Heads and other leaders need to keep a sense of balance between such things as formality and informality, collecting information and views and acting on them, pressure and support. You may rarely get the balance 'right', but it is important to avoid getting it very wrong.

Chapters 1 to 3 have looked at the need for heads to provide leadership in the school. In the next chapter we will look at the different kinds of leadership heads need to think about.

Chapter 4
Leadership

Leadership is one of those words which is used a great deal without being very clearly defined. Indeed, a massive amount of research has been conducted into leadership, but it hasn't always resulted in greater clarity. This chapter will begin with a brief description of what leadership means. This will be followed by a review of six types of leadership, all of which are relevant to leadership in primary schools.

It's important to understand that there are different types of leadership and that these types all play a part in determining the success of a school. Therefore, as you read through the definitions – especially the types of leadership described here – you might want to ask yourself the following questions.

- Who provides this type of leadership in our school?
- How often is such leadership offered?
- When was the last time such leadership was exercised?
- Which type is the most common or prevalent in our school?
- How might we further develop each type of leadership in the school?

What is leadership?

There is a distinction between management and leadership. Broadly speaking, management is concerned with the smooth running of the school. Leadership is to do with developing the school.

Leaders help to provide a sense of direction – they help us all to see where we are going, why we are heading in that direction and how we will get there.

Sometimes leaders take decisions by themselves in order to help the group move forward. Often they involve members of the group they are leading in the decision-making process. Leaders are both decisive and consultative and see those qualities as two sides of the same coin.

Leaders are essentially action-orientated. They are reflective, analytic and strategic thinkers, but they also get things done.

Leaders strive to improve the quality of the school. Therefore, they are developers and leaders of change and it is during times of change that leadership is most visible because that is when it is needed most. If you and your colleagues are striving to improve aspects of your school, then you need to provide, and to be seen to provide, leadership.

Someone has to help the group see the direction in which they are heading and to make things happen to move the group towards that goal. That is what leaders do.

Types of leadership

Out of the countless types and styles of leadership which have been categorised during a century of research, six are especially important for leadership in school.

Chapter 4 **Leadership**

1 Situational leadership

Simply stated, this type of leadership recognises that where you are affects what you do. Consider the following examples:

> Park Street Primary School is located in an inner city urban area where there is much poverty. The school buildings are old, they leak and are in need of redecoration and repair. The children at Key Stage 1 are housed in a separate block from those at Key Stage 2. Equipment is in poor condition and teaching materials are scarce. The governors are very concerned about the quality of the teaching. Staff morale is low. There are 325 pupils in the school.

> The Cedars Primary School is situated in a suburban location next to a green belt on the edge of a county town. The school was built eight years ago and the accommodation is attractive and colourful. The fabric of the building is good. The governors are very supportive of the work of the school and a recent inspection has praised the school for the quality of the work achieved by the children. Staff morale is high. There are 145 pupils in the school.

A new head arriving at Park Street School would have a rather different job to do from that of a new head at the Cedars School. This is because the size and location of the school can influence the leader's priorities.

Of course, there are many other factors which will impinge upon the nature of leadership, for example

- staff morale
- the image of the school
- the type of school (eg. infant, infant and nursery, junior, JMI, primary, as well as whether the school is an LEA school, GM, or church-aided or controlled)

- the age and experience of the staff
- the skills and qualities of other leaders in the school (especially the deputy and the coordinators)
- the state of the school's finances
- how much ancillary support is available for the head
- the needs of the pupils (levels of achievement, SEN, the progress pupils are making).

If where you are affects what you do as a head then it follows that heads need to be able to

- take stock of the school's situation and circumstances
- analyse the situational evidence
- devise relevant and school-specific strategies and action plans
- monitor the implementation of the action plans
- review and revise as progress is made over time.

The last point is very important. A year into your headship, the situation will have altered. New priorities will emerge and a sense of progress should be shared with staff. Situational leadership involves not only analysis but also flexible planning. For this reason, school development planning must form an important part of a head's leadership and management strategies.

Situational leadership is really about ensuring that your approach to leading the school meets the school's circumstances and needs. Effective leaders tailor their actions to the demands they face, as well as to the goals they are seeking to achieve. Effective heads are constantly monitoring what's happening in and around the school. They look carefully at these perceptions, check them with others – especially the deputy, senior staff and the chair of governors – and, in the light of this monitoring and evaluation, decide upon the action steps needed.

Chapter 4 **Leadership**

2 Instrumental leadership

This type of leadership and expressive leadership – which follows – are closely connected. Although each is examined on its own, heads need to think about how they work together in a school. As you read through them ask yourself the question, 'Who is providing instrumental leadership and who is providing expressive leadership in your school?'

Instrumental leadership is concerned with getting the job done. In schools this means, for example, ensuring that there is quality teaching and learning, that records are kept, that the curriculum is in place and operational. It is task-centred leadership.

It is leadership where the deputy, coordinator or subject manager, as well as the head, give a lead on such things as classroom management, the pace and challenge of work offered in classrooms, assessing rates of pupil progress, how the curriculum is organised and how quality in all these matters (and many more) will be judged.

Instrumental leaders ensure that things happen in terms of the fundamental purpose of the school – teaching children and ensuring that appropriate learning for all is taking place. They don't settle for what is customarily offered, but try to help individuals and work teams achieve even better results.

3 Expressive leadership

Expressive leadership is concerned with a sense of consideration for others and the affective and pastoral needs of colleagues and others. It takes account of the well-being of colleagues, their personal concerns and professional challenges.

Expressive leaders help to prevent the organisation from becoming too oppressive and too task centred. They ensure that individuals and groups feel their work and commitments are recognised and appreciated. Moreover, they empathise with others. They try to listen to colleagues' views and to develop a whole-school perspective by gathering in the perceptions of everyone in the team. They are receptive to alternative ideas because they value what others have to say, even when those views are contrary to their own.

Expressive leaders care about their colleagues as people and persons in their own right.

Chapter 3 concluded by stressing the importance of a sensible balance between these two kinds of leadership. Too much instrumental leadership can create a sense of being driven and of the school being an organisation where no attention is paid to the needs of individuals. On the other hand, too much expressive leadership can breed a sense of indulgence, complacency or cosiness.

Instrumental and expressive leadership might be likened to leaders needing to show a blend of toughness and tenderness.

Another way of approaching these two types of leadership is to think about how leaders in a school collectively provide a mix of the two. One leader might offer more instrumental and less expressive leadership. Another might counterbalance this by providing more expressive and pastoral support. Nias (1987) researched and analysed the way a head and deputy partnership in an infant and nursery school operated and applied the idea of instrumental and expressive leadership to them. It's an interesting account and offers a model for how others might reflect on leadership in their own schools.

Chapter 4 **Leadership**

4 Cultural leadership

Every school has its own organisational culture. Culture refers to the 'way we do things around here'. It's made up of the values, habits, customs and procedures by which a group of adults work together and interact with one another.

If you think about different schools in which you've worked, you might recognise how in each school you and your colleagues did things slightly differently. For example, patterns of staff meetings vary between schools. The way meetings are conducted is different. In some schools, it's accepted that you debate and challenge each other. In others, such discussions might be regarded as too confrontational.

Culture determines how staff work together, what relations between teachers are like, whether teachers visit one another and observe each other at work, whether there is collegial support or not, whether staff challenge each other, recognise one another's successes, feel they are part of a team or work on their own in isolation.

Culture is also about how staff look after one another. Whether they share ideas, support one another, talk to each other and have some fun. In some schools, not only is there very little peer contact and discussion, there is also no humour. In other schools, there is much more joke telling and light-heartedness. Some schools are 'cold' places to work in, others are exceedingly 'warm' organisations. This kind of 'climatic' difference is produced by the school's organisational culture.

Culture is a powerful feature of school life. It creates and sustains workplace conditions which in turn contribute to whether the school is a place of independent action, comfortable inertia or collaborative development.

To understand the idea more thoroughly you might look at Fullan and Hargreaves (1992) and Nias *et al.* (1989).

In terms of leadership, headteachers play an important part in establishing and maintaining particular kinds of culture. Heads, therefore, need to be mindful that all their actions impinge in myriad ways upon the school's culture.

For example, heads who always make decisions on their own are signalling that professional independence is what matters. By contrast, heads who consult are demonstrating that interdependence is important. The latter will be contributing to a stronger sense of teamwork and collaboration and be supporting a sense of whole school.

Culture is a difficult concept because it's not one thing but lots of ways of doing things. Whilst every act is important, some are more important than others. For example, what heads say in school assemblies, how they conduct meetings, how much attention they give to others, to teams, to success and to challenge, are all significant matters because such actions symbolise the value of them. Staff 'read' these actions and draw two things from them

- whether the leader's actions are consistent with her words
- the actual value of these activities relative to other aspects of school life and work.

In other words, heads provide a personal and professional example which influences others and fashions how they, in turn, will behave.

Chapter 4 **Leadership**

5 Transactional leadership

The work of a headteacher involves a great deal of time and effort being expended on keeping the school ticking over. Essentially, this means that the head, along with the school's secretary, clerical assistants and bursar (if you are fortunate to have this position in your school) will be busily engaged in managing the school site, plant and equipment as well as coping with the day-to-day issues. For example, there will be parents to meet, prospective parents to show around the school, governors to consult, children to attend to, messages to deal with and so on. Anything from lost property to correspondence from the DfEE may make calls upon your time.

All of this is important and much of it will be necessary. Of course, from time to time, every head needs to review whether she is doing too much of this kind of work. Such a review is necessary because someone else might be able to do these things and thus free you to engage with more professional and educational concerns. Administration and organisational affairs are a legitimate call upon a head's time, but the proportion of the time they take up needs to be monitored closely.

Administration and office commitments can be a trap where you feel you are very busy but mightn't be contributing to the development of the teaching and learning in the school. In this way, heads can be in the middle of things but not always at the heart of the school.

Transactional leadership is necessary, but it's not all there is to leading a school. In order to be effective, things in the school need to 'work'. Materials and equipment should be plentiful and in good order. There should be structures and systems for dealing with finances, policies, requisitions, communications, meetings and curriculum developments. These and many other things enable the school to function reasonably smoothly and efficiently.

All of this might simply sound like straightforward management. A lot of it is, but there's a leadership dimension to such management because, as head, you need to consider what kind of organisation you want.

Transactional leaders use their everyday tasks and administrative duties as the means by which they create and sustain the particular kind of school organisation they want. They may, for example, give a lead in listening to what visitors have to say and to paying attention to the views of others, especially parents. To do this they might ensure that telephones aren't left ringing but are answered quickly and that letters and notes from parents are responded to promptly. They might set up a clear reception area for visitors to the school. They will send out questionnaires and response sheets to check out parental views. They might meet regularly with the parent governors and discuss, informally, emerging concerns and ideas from groups of parents. They might approach every face-to-face complaint as an opportunity to persuade someone of the validity of the school's aims and philosophy and as a chance to turn a detractor into a supporter of the school.

Yet, while transactional leadership ensures the school is properly maintained and is an effective organisation which promotes certain key principles, there is also a need for development. Hence, transactional leadership needs to be seen alongside a measure of transformational leadership.

Chapter 4 **Leadership**

6 Transformational leadership

As the title suggests, this type of leadership is about moving the school on. Transactional leadership provides the stability and continuity for the school to operate efficiently. Transformational leadership builds upon this maintenance function. It uses the relatively stable platform of a well-organised school and simultaneously strives for some initiative-taking and development work. Transformational leadership is simply about transforming aspects of the school. It is leadership which contributes to school improvement.

Such leadership is concerned with the management of change (see Fullan, 1991). It's closely connected with the priorities and targets identified in the school's development plan.

This type of leadership is also concerned with empowering colleagues. Such leadership isn't always leadership from the front. It's less about 'gung ho' charges and heroic leadership and more to do with encouraging others.

The notion of transformation is a kind of metaphor. If we think of transformers in an electrical sense, then what a transformer does is up the voltage of others. (yes... they also decrease the voltage of others, but we'll ignore that side of things here!) Taken in this positive sense, transformational leaders up the voltage of others. They increase the contribution and commitment of colleagues. They are effective leaders because they increase the effectiveness of others.

Heads, therefore, need to offer a blend of transactional and transformational leadership and need to consider the balance between the two types. Similarly, you need to review how expressive and instrumental leadership is distributed in the school, who is providing cultural leadership and how specific all of this is to the school's circumstances and needs.

By way of closing this chapter, it's worth reiterating that these six types of leadership provide a useful framework of ideas to analyse leadership in your school. The questions cited on page 25 are useful tools for beginning to reflect on the nature, distribution and patterns of leadership in your own school. They are especially useful to consider in relation to how you and your deputy operate as a pair of leaders. This theme is also developed in the next chapter where working with your deputy is examined.

Chapter 5
Working with your deputy

There are many dangers and pitfalls in headship. One is that heads think that they're indispensable. Another is that they think that they're the sole leader in the school. Neither is true and both should be avoided. There are many leaders in schools. Some are informal leaders, these are the influential individuals who others respect, look to for an opinion or who might intimidate colleagues. Others are formal leaders, having been coordinators and year leaders. Deputies, of course, come within this latter group, although they can also be important informal leaders as well, especially if they're not fully involved as a formal leader. This chapter focusses on how to involve the deputy.

The involvement of the deputy is important. Not only does it make managerial sense for heads to share out some of their responsibilities, but also when deputies are involved and work closely with the head, the school is more effective. Research into effective schools shows that one of the characteristics associated with more successful schools is that the head and the deputy work together (Mortimore *et al* 1988).

Many heads and deputies recognise this fact and have developed productive partnerships. Some heads and deputies, however, have not. Often the lack of a partnership is attributed to the inability of the head and deputy to 'get on'. This difficulty is understandable – there is always going to be an element of human chemistry in the relationship – sometimes this outlook is based too strongly on social factors and not enough on professional relations.

Let's look at an example. A patient undergoing surgery in a hospital probably doesn't care whether the surgeon likes the anaesthetist or not. However, during the operation the patient is right to expect that the two consultants are able to work together. Much the same is true of pupils and parents. They may not need the head and deputy to like one another, but they are entitled to expect that the two work together to better serve the children and the school as a whole.

Naturally, it helps if the two relate well to one another, but the point is that they should work together – it's a professional partnership they are trying to create and not a social one. Interpersonal differences should be set aside, as far as possible, and the two must strive to develop effective ways of working alongside each other because it has been shown that professional partnerships make schools more effective.

The first thing to establish, then, is that working with the deputy is a professional partnership. Now we can turn to the principles and characteristics which enable such partnerships to flourish.

Some recent work in one LEA has focussed on the principles which are needed to guide the work and contribution of deputy heads. The following principles were developed by a group of deputies working with an LEA inspector.

Chapter 5 **Working with your deputy**

Principles of deputy headship

Deputies need

- a positive partnership with the heads
- to play a major role – in collaboration with the head – in formulating the aims and objectives of the school, establishing the policies through which they will be achieved and monitoring progress
- planned preparation for deputising, acting headship and headship
- an entitlement to some non-contact and quality time
- to promote the values of the school to the community and stakeholders
- to manage specific responsibilities delegated to them
- the authority to delegate duties and tasks to other colleagues
- to review regularly the balance of class teaching responsibilities and school management duties.

(Hertfordshire Education Services, 1994)

These principles are helpful in that they make it clear what is expected of deputies as well as what heads need to attend to so that they can be partners.

It follows that the deputy should have a job description, which should be drawn up in consultation with her. The head and deputy should jointly review their respective roles and negotiate a job description which reflects

- the needs of the school, including priorities in the school's development plan
- the strengths and experience of the deputy
- the development needs of the deputy
- the deputy's teaching commitments

- the head's role and current priorities
- the support needs of other colleagues.

During the framing of the deputy's job description attention might also be paid to the principles set out on page 39.

Together, the principles and the job description begin to set parameters on what the deputy and head might do. However, they don't demonstrate how they need to operate jointly.

Characteristics of successful head and deputy partnerships

Little is known about how heads and deputies actually work together. There have been few studies of this subject but some small-scale studies can be used to throw a little light on the it. The following characteristics have been identified by heads and deputies who have been perceived to be members of successful partnerships. They were categorised by a group of deputies in Hertfordshire who investigated what heads and deputies did when they worked well together (see also Southworth, 1994 and 1995). The following eight characteristics were identified in the study.

1 A shared philosophy

There was agreement between the two partners on the academic, social and moral goals for the school, as well as shared understanding about how the school should be organised. This means that heads and deputies need to talk about their respective educational and organisational values and work out what they agree on and where they might have to agree to differ.

Chapter 5 **Working with your deputy**

2 Professional and personal respect

Each partner needs to value and respect the other's judgments and opinions. The key word is respect – that means what it says. They don't need to like or agree with each other's views, but should respect them. Both partners need to recognise that the other might disagree and change their ideas and actions and shouldn't be surprised when she does. On matters where agreement and solidarity are essential, they will need to be discussed and rehearsed.

3 Trust

Trust comes from sharing ideas, being frank and honest with one another and, when heads delegate to deputies, letting them carry out the task without interfering. Heads must let deputies do things on their own. They should avoid being seen as meddlesome.

Trust is also developed when individuals behave consistently. It is very difficult to trust someone when you don't know how they will react because they keep changing their view or have rapid mood swings. For trust to grow and flourish, a reasonable measure of consistency in how you behave towards each other is needed.

4 Heads aware of deputies' lack of time

Teaching deputies have a difficult dual role to perform. They are usually full-time class teachers who also have to fulfil important management and development tasks. Ideally deputies should have at least some release time. A head might, for example, cover the deputy's class every now and then. By providing the deputy with some release time, the head is signalling to the deputy and to the school as a whole that the role of the deputy is an important one. Time is a precious commodity in school. How it's used symbolises the importance of what it is given to. If no time is given to the deputy, it might be interpreted as meaning that the deputy is unimportant.

5 Both aware of the school's situation

Both the heads and deputies in the successful partnerships related their roles to the school's specific circumstances. In a sense, this is sound situational leadership as discussed in the previous chapter. In other words, the work of the head and the deputy needs to be based upon the school's needs. What drives such partnerships is less the wishes of the head and the deputy and more what needs to be done to maintain and develop the school. For these reasons, the school's development plan forms an important part of the partnership.

6 Active, frequent and regular communication

In successful partnerships it's understood that in order to work closely together both partners need to be in regular contact. There must be free-flowing communication. This includes

- regular but short meetings
- frequent briefing sessions to update one another
- informal professional talk
- touring the school together
- the head keeping an in-tray for the deputy so that they have shared knowledge of messages, memos and the mail.

There is also a case for the head and deputy to have some extended time together to think strategically about the school, evaluate performance and plan ahead.

Chapter 5 **Working with your deputy**

7 Not an exclusive partnership

One danger of working closely with someone is that other colleagues can feel excluded. To avoid this, heads and deputies need to try to involve others, be they members of the senior management team or teaching colleagues. Open meetings are a good way to allow those colleagues who might wish to join in to do so. It's also important that the head and deputy consult with colleagues. Both should try to prevent their partnership becoming a 'separate entity' within the school. If it does it is likely to inhibit any sense of a whole school being developed.

8 Accept differences

In any partnership there are bound to be some differences, the issue is how are they handled. Differences are healthy and often creative – so long as they are regarded as differences. Unfortunately, some people see difference as deviance. When differences occur they need to be faced, discussed and resolved. It's best to avoid harbouring differences – try to talk them through. Here the need for active, frequent and regular communication is most important.

Hopefully, these eight characteristics will help you to form a productive partnership. However, in closing this chapter, it's worth offering some practical ways in which partnerships have been developed.

In a number of schools the names of both the head *and* the deputy appear on the school's official headed notepaper. This seemingly small gesture is in fact a significant symbol both of partnership and the deputy's status.

Another example is how some deputies have been retitled and

are called 'assistant heads'. This is intended to signal that the deputy is not waiting to play a part only when the head is absent, but that the deputy is constantly involved in the running of the school by assisting the head.

A third idea is that the deputy is given opportunities to lead when the head is present. All too often, deputies lead only when the head is away or detained elsewhere. It's a more powerful example of joint leadership when, from time to time, the deputy chairs a meeting, leads a workshop or speaks to parents and governors when the head is present. The challenge here is for the head to avoid being a 'back seat driver'. When it works, the arrangement is a potent indicator of the deputy's status and contribution. It's a real sign of joint and shared leadership.

Put simply, partnership between a head and deputy is based on the adage that 'two heads are better than one'. Shared leadership is likely to be more effective, given that the above principles and characteristics are put into practice. Importantly, shared leadership is not cloning but two perspectives combining to enrich the school's development and management. When there is a powerful partnership, the two – along with other school leaders – should be better placed to influence the teaching and learning in the school.

At the heart of school management and leadership is a strong and constant concern to improve the quality of teaching and learning. Chapter 6 sets out the ways in which a head can influence teaching in a school.

Chapter 6
Ways of influencing teaching

The advent of self-managing schools, increased powers and involvement of school governors, the reduction in the role of the LEA GM status, and the implementation of a National Curriculum have all helped to create the circumstances in which heads can become preoccupied with administrative and managerial concerns at the expense of their attention to teaching.

Many heads are now trying to refocus some of their attention on teaching and learning across the whole school, not least because school inspections concentrate on the quality of the teaching in the school and standards of pupils' attainments. A head's capacity to influence teaching is a high priority.

Traditionally, it has been common for heads to influence teaching in 'their' schools by leading by example. For many this has meant teaching regularly each week (where they have a choice in the matter). This is a useful option but it's necessary to consider additional ways of influencing teaching in a school.

The following ideas are drawn from the practice of experienced heads. They aren't presented in order of priority, and it isn't an exhaustive treatment of the subject. There are many ways of influencing teaching, these are but some ideas which are offered as a spur to your thinking.

Talk about teaching and learning

There's no shortage of topics to discuss and deal with in schools today. At any one time there is usually something to be debated and talked through. One consequence of this is that it's all too easy for the core concerns to be taken for granted – for teaching and learning issues to be overlooked. To counter such oversights, heads need to make a conscious effort to make time to talk with colleagues in school about teaching and learning.

This seemingly obvious task involves at least three aspects.

First, heads and other senior teachers need to ensure that there is a frequent and regular opportunity for them to create a dialogue with colleagues about what is going on in classrooms.

Second, heads need to be clear that the discussions they have with colleagues are about teaching and learning. The use of these two terms is quite deliberate and fundamental. By stressing teaching and learning, rather than curriculum, the intention is to emphasise that these conversations should focus on what teachers are actually teaching and how. Pedagogy should be one part of the discussion. The other part should be what children are doing and learning. The following are some of the questions likely to be raised and addressed during these conversations.

- How are individual pupils progressing?
- What are the concerns of the teacher?
- How are groups of children working together?
- How are particular school policies (eg. special needs/equal opportunities policies) being implemented?

Third, while such dialogue is important, it is vital that the head listens as well as talks. In effect, these conversations are a way of monitoring what's happening in classrooms.

Chapter 6 **Ways of influencing teaching**

Visit teachers in their classrooms

Dialogue needs to be supported and nourished by visits to the classrooms and other teaching areas. One head I know keeps an afternoon a week clear to be able to visit classrooms and join in with whatever is taking place. This head believes it's important to ensure that some time is regularly dedicated to this activity, so that she knows what's happening around the school. Moreover, she doesn't rely on informal opportunities alone because she regards these as too *ad hoc,* and they do not guarantee that all teacher colleagues will be visited.

Another head ensures that each week she uses at least one after-school period, from around 3.30 to 5.30 to visit her colleagues and talk over what they have been doing that day and week.

In both these examples, as with the first suggestion, there's a measure of monitoring taking place. However, in neither case is the intention to supervise the teachers. Instead, both heads use this time to keep in touch with classroom concerns, to demonstrate a continuing interest in these matters and to recognise, value and praise their colleagues' efforts. They are monitoring not to check up on people but, as one head said, 'to catch colleagues doing something well'.

Manage by wandering about

It is important that the head walks around the school as a whole and sees how it looks, watches what's going on and listens to what's being said, sung and acted out. Managers in many workplaces know the value of informal tours around the site. Management by wandering about, or MBWA, is really no more than touring the workplace and developing one's professional skills of perception. In effect it's a form of school-based enquiry and evaluation. Again, it allows judgments to be made using first-hand knowledge of what's happening. It enables patterns to be detected and then shared with colleagues.

For example, one head who tours her school a lot, was able over half a term to note the absence of poetry across the school. She then informally raised this observation with year group leaders and the senior management team. Then, she shared her perception with all the staff and initiated a debate about the place of poetry in the curriculum and the frequency with which it should be used. Similar observations could be made about the visual arts, 3D work, information technology, the development of independence in children, behaviour management, drama in the school and so on.

Encourage staff to visit one another

Visits by the head demonstrate her strong interest in teaching and learning and concern about the quality of what's happening across the school, but others need to visit classrooms too. It's surprising how little inter-classroom visiting takes place in some schools. Sometimes the design and layout of the building inhibits visits, sometimes teachers of older children fail to visit teachers of younger pupils or vice versa. Every school has its own norms and patterns concerning whether staff visit one another, with what frequency and for what purposes.

In a truly 'open' school, where there are no barriers to visiting one another and no interpersonal tensions, staff might visit in order to

- be aware of what everyone is teaching each half term
- develop consistent approaches to classroom management and organisation

Chapter 6 **Ways of influencing teaching**

- establish and sustain consistent approaches to behaviour management
- focus on how curriculum subjects are taught by each teacher
- develop a range of teaching styles
- conduct action research into aspects of one another's classroom practice.

There's no shortage of possibilities. And, without doubt, one of the most powerful ways of developing teachers is by enabling them to see what their colleagues are doing.

Although, in some schools, this proposal might be a radical departure from established patterns of interaction, the idea need not be implemented on its own. There are several other initiatives which have facilitated classroom observation and these should be used as ways of establishing the pattern. These initiatives include teacher appraisal, mentoring for newly qualified teachers, agreement trialling in assessment and 'showing' assemblies, when teachers take turns to show the rest of the school examples of the activities their classes have been engaged in.

Use INSET days and sessions to focus on teaching

While there's no shortage of issues to address in school, there is a need to devote some of the staff's collective INSET time every year to focussing on teaching. Questions such as the following could be used to encourage colleagues to reflect on their approaches and to develop common ways of working across the school.

- How are we teaching reading?
- Are we using higher order questions in classrooms?

- Are we using cooperative groups for learning?

The central issue here is how and when staff collectively reflect on what they are doing in the classroom. And the key word here is 'reflect'. The intention shouldn't be to evaluate an individual teacher's ways of working, much less to judge or criticise. The aim is rather to ask questions of one's own approach and to learn with and from others about how they are tackling the same concerns. In the light of such reflection some agreements might be established and policies created. However, first and foremost, staff need the opportunity to discuss and think about what and how they are teaching.

Discuss pupils

In addition to reflecting upon teaching, it's necessary and useful to encourage staff to talk about individuals, groups and classes of pupils. For some staff it will be easier and a little less threatening to talk about children than to examine their teaching in the company of colleagues. However, by inviting teachers in staff meetings, year groups and key stage teams to consider how the children are progressing, and to look at individual cases, you are effectively

- creating sharing and openness between colleagues
- providing opportunities for colleagues to benefit from each others' advice
- developing a professional approach and response to children's needs
- enabling staff to agree action points and plans for pupils
- moving towards the position where every child is seen as having special needs
- encouraging strong teamwork and mutual self help
- promoting a healthy and vital attention to pupils' learning.

Chapter 6 **Ways of influencing teaching**

Develop clarity about what effective teaching means

Another important way of influencing teachers is to establish within the school an agreed and shared view about effective teaching. In some schools, the heads have set out personal statements of what they believe constitutes 'good classroom practice'. In other schools, there are whole-school policies for teaching.

A useful starting point is to invite colleagues to try to set out for themselves what they think a good teacher is like. They might try to describe a teacher whose practice they admire. Or small groups of staff might try to sketch out the key professional characteristics of a 'good teacher'. Such portraits could then be used to generate discussion and debate.

Alternatively, there is now a lot of useful material available which could easily be used as stimulus or source material to focus staff meetings, INSET days or position papers. One readily available source is the OFSTED *Handbook for School Inspections* with its criteria for teaching. You might also consider inviting an OFSTED Inspector, an LEA officer or someone from a university or college Department of Education to lead a staff discussion on the topic.

Look at classroom environments

In some schools each term begins with teachers being given some time the day before school opens to set up their classrooms for the work to be covered. Then all the staff tour the school, as a group, visiting each classroom in turn. The group will spend time looking at how the classroom has been set up and then the teacher will explain to her colleagues what is going to be taught that term or half-term, how the room has been set up and ask for further suggestions and comments. Often staff can offer help with specific topics or pieces of equipment and materials and gradually introduce helpful comments along the lines of 'Why don't you try this?' or 'Did you think of putting this there?'

These visits encourage teachers to look and think carefully about their classrooms, to benefit from the suggestions and support of colleagues and to see how others are going about planning and preparing their classrooms.

Additionally, such visits encourage whole-school approaches to display and classroom organisation to be developed and implemented, since everyone sees everybody else's efforts.

Concluding thoughts

These seemingly straightforward ideas will, separately and together, help

- to develop and influence the ways teachers work in their classrooms
- teachers create the conditions whereby they can learn from their colleagues (seé Chapter 4)
- to establish a culture of collaboration and professional learning.
- the head to keep in touch with what's happening in the school as a whole as well as in individual classrooms.

Research into effective schools suggests that one characteristic of successful schools is that the staff in them, especially the senior staff, take a strong interest in teaching and learning. These ideas will ensure that this happens. Also, a current school development project in the USA shows that teachers and others need to be relentless in their quest for

Chapter 6 **Ways of influencing teaching**

quality if they are to improve their teaching. Successful teaching relies on persistent hard work and endeavour – and the same is true of headship.

If a head wants to influence teaching across the school she needs to apply and reapply these and other ideas with a relentless persistence. By so doing she will be opening up the school, increasing awareness amongst staff and spreading the best practice of individuals across the whole school.

However, there is one other point to note. These seemingly straightforward strategies for influencing teaching rely upon reasonably healthy interpersonal relations. Staff need to see classroom visits, staff discussion and the head working alongside them as professional opportunities for development and not as supervision or, worse, surveillance. Most of these processes are concerned with professional learning whereby everyone learns with and from one another – where each individual contributes to colleagues' development and, in turn, gains from others. In order for this to happen, staff must be able to work well with one another. In this respect, the head needs to lead by example. Heads must be able to work well with colleagues, which is why Chapter 7 is linked closely to this chapter.

Chapter 7
Working with others

Schools are people-intensive places. They aren't factories staffed by robots, controlled by computers and directed by a few managers who follow manuals from head office. First and foremost, schools are human places.

Because schools are social organisations they are special places. They're one of the main settings, outside of the family, in which children learn about social behaviour, customs and rules. Therefore, how people relate to one another isn't simply a matter of social relations, it's a vital part of a child's social education. In other words, how adults relate to one another, as well as how they relate to children, is an important part of the school's curriculum.

This 'social fact' of schooling has important implications for how heads work with colleagues. Staff relations are significant not only because they influence the effectiveness of the workplace, but also because how adults behave with one another is noticed by pupils and has a bearing upon how children perceive and understand interpersonal relations. Schools might not always be model communities, but they do demonstrate to children how adults relate to one another at work – be it positively or negatively. In this way, schools tacitly – but powerfully – transmit messages about such things as collegiality, authority and subordination. Schools are places

Chapter 7 **Working with others**

where children begin to develop a sense of democracy or autocracy as well as of interdependence or isolation.

Therefore, notions such as a positive organisational 'culture of collaboration' (Nias *et al* 1989) or a sense of 'total schools' worth fighting for (Fullan and Hargreaves.1992) are important, because they offer children a chance to see adults working productively together and provide them with constructive models of how workplaces can be both social and moral places.

Such aspirations need to be borne in mind when heads reflect upon how they work with colleagues and how they expect colleagues to work with others, because the everyday transactions between head and staff are the medium and the message of social and moral behaviour.

What does this mean for heads? Given that everyday life contains moral overtones and undertones, it needs to be recognised that almost every action and transaction is significant. Heads not only have to describe and articulate how they want colleagues to work together, but also demonstrate good practice in their own deeds. In this respect, heads are exemplars. Heads, in common with other leaders, must set an example.

This chapter looks at four key aspects of organisational relations in schools

- professional relations
- valuing others
- involving governors
- micropolitics.

Professional relations

The purpose of schools is to educate children. For this to happen, teachers and other members of staff need to relate productively with one another. Hopefully, staff will be able to get along with one another at a social level. However, it's important that staff can work together. This doesn't mean that staff need necessarily like one another. It does mean that they must be able to talk professionally, to share information and jointly plan and implement policies.

These requirements are implied when teachers and heads acknowledge that there must be a reasonable degree of consultation between staff, that the curriculum needs to be coordinated and that there has to be a measure of curriculum continuity across the school.

In developing and sustaining productive working relations, heads need to emphasise the professional reasons and benefits of inter-staff collaboration. Heads need to help teachers (whose first concern is always the classroom and 'their' class) that working with colleagues isn't a distraction from classroom matters but, rather, a necessary part of making the school and each classroom more effective for the children.

So heads must exemplify to staff that collaboration is important professionally. They shouldn't emphasise social interaction at the expense of professional discourse. Heads must encourage teachers and other staff members to talk about their work.

Valuing others

One of the ways in which heads can foster professional openness is by making everyone feel valued. Heads are usually very good at praising colleagues' efforts and

Chapter 7 **Working with others**

achievements and this is clearly one important strategy. However, praise must be sincere, and so can't be used too liberally.

Alongside appreciating colleagues' efforts, a genuine interest in what colleagues have to say about their work is needed. One of the best ways of valuing someone is to listen to them. It's evidence that you're paying attention to someone else and an investment of your time. It gives the message that you are consultative and interested in the views, ideas and perceptions of individuals.

Listening isn't easy – it's hard work. It's also made more difficult because heads and teachers are inveterate talkers. And talking isn't always good preparation for listening. Teachers and heads might be better speakers than listeners.

The type of attention referred to here is called 'active listening'. The following skills of active listening are offered as an *aide memoire*. Heads who use them are usually more successful in developing and maintaining professional standards of consultation and collaboration.

Skills of active listening

The key word is ACTIVE. Active listening doesn't mean sitting quietly and patiently waiting for the speaker to finish. Active listening involves finding out what the speaker is saying and feeling. This means that the listener needs to check with the speaker

- what was consciously communicated
- that what she received was what was intended to be sent
- whether there were any distortions in what was sent and received.

To achieve this, the listener needs to check, from time to time, what is being conveyed. The listener should try to paraphrase what has been said so far:

> 'As I see it, what you are saying is...'

and encourage the speaker to amplify and clarify some points:

> 'Tell me a bit more about what happened when...'

> 'So what followed from that meeting...?'

Once the message has been understood, the next stage is to consider the implications of what's being stated

> 'Would that mean that...?'

> 'So how might that idea work here...?'

Next, it is sometimes helpful to reflect the underlying feelings of the speaker

> 'Did you feel rather anxious about...?'

> 'If that happened to me I'd be rather upset...'

Following this exploration of the topic, the listener needs to summarise what's been said in a couple of sentences. This can sometimes help to bring the dialogue to a close, or can lead on to some action points being discussed.

As well as the listener interjecting in these ways, non-verbal responses are important – eye-contact, nodding and other receptive signals.

The listener needs to aim for an 80/20 balance – listen for 80 per cent of the time, talk for no more than 20 per cent.

Chapter 7 **Working with others**

Involving governors

As well as working with members of staff, heads need to involve the school's governors. There are many ways of doing this and one of the first things a head might do in this area is talk to other heads about how they try to work with governors. The following points might also provide food for thought.

Keep the governors informed. Plan your report to governors so that it's informative. Describe what has been happening in the school, promote the successes of the school, teachers and pupils.

Give the governors tasks to do. In some schools individual governors are attached to individual classes and encouraged to visit. The children keep them informed at update meetings or by newsletters. Parent governors could contribute to the school's newsletters to parents. Sometimes, there are visiting governors. Each term, one or two governors spend part of a day in the school focussing on an aspect of the school and then reporting back to the other governors at the next full meeting.

Keep the chair of governors informed. Set up regular face-to-face meetings. If you can, include the deputy in these meetings. Ensure that relevant copies of letters, newsletters and invitations to school events are sent to all governors.

As a prelude to governor meetings, invite them to tour the school and to look at the work on display.

When governors visit informally, let some of the children show them around the school.

Micropolitics

Schools are political places. The politics of the local community, the parish pump and the 'school gate mafia' (as one beleaguered head called them!) are part and parcel of running a school. There might also be interpersonal and interprofessional tensions between colleagues. Heads need to manage these tensions.

There are just three things to note here. First, the actions and words of the head are always significant. As a head you need to think of yourself as always being 'on stage'. In a sense, you have to try to play to various audiences. Most importantly, though, remember you are being watched and your actions observed. Heads are visible people. It's important not only to be consistent, fair and to listen to others but to be seen to be doing those things.

Second, you need to watch your words. You should be diplomatic about what you say and to whom. A few casual or incautious remarks can lead to all kinds of local incidents.

Third, when working with others, bear in mind that you will be involved in overt and covert negotiations. Colleagues will sometimes try to manipulate you, as will other stakeholders. From time to time, you might find yourself manipulating them. Manipulation is fraught and often dangerous, not least because it undermines open professional relations. Try to avoid putting yourself, your colleagues (especially the deputy) and the school in a position from which it's difficult to extricate yourselves.

Whenever possible, try to give yourself some thinking time. Then you can reflect on the implications of what might be needed, consider other options and prepare how to present

Chapter 7 **Working with others**

your ideas and responses. It's not always possible to do this, but when you can it's often a valuable tactic.

Headship is a tough job. Working with so many other people, and to so many different agendas and schedules is stressful and demanding. Headship takes its toll on heads. You might want to look at Chapter 8 and consider how to manage yourself.

Chapter 8
Managing yourself

Headship can be a strain, it can even be stressful (see Southworth, 1995). Heads need to look after themselves if they are to perform their roles effectively and efficiently.

This chapter reviews three sets of issues

- organisation
- professional development
- personal time.

Organisation

Heads need to be well-organised. A disorganised head is not only individually inefficient, but will also make others ineffective. A school secretary who has to wait while the head searches for lost papers is being prevented from getting on with her duties. One of the biggest areas of complaint from secretaries, as well as from others, about their 'bosses', is when they prevent or delay them from getting on. Inefficient people are a nuisance and a source of frustration to others.

Being organised means having a list of what needs to be done today and having an efficient filing system which the deputy and secretary also understand and can 'work'. It means planning ahead and anticipating deadlines. It also means being prepared.

Chapter 8 **Managing yourself**

There are no magic formulae to save the disorganised. It's more a matter of developing systems which work for you and others.

One important area is that of time management. There are numerous books about how to improve in this area. *Primary File* has also published some helpful advice about it (Time Management by M. Skelton, issues 12 and 13, 1991). It is useful periodically to review how you are using time and ask yourself the following questions.

- Is this a good use of my time?
- Could someone else do this?
- How can I help others to do these things?

Time management all too often relates to delegation.

Many heads find delegation difficult, usually for two reasons. First, the time it takes to delegate is often greater than if you do it yourself. However, this is really only a short-term solution. In the long run it is a trap which makes you keep on doing those things which others should be doing.

Second, heads often find it hard to let go of responsibilities. You have to – indeed, you already have. The most important thing in a school is teaching and learning and that has already been handed over, at least in part, to the teaching staff. By comparison, everything else should be easy to delegate.

If heads don't let go of many of their responsibilities, they could become submerged and overwhelmed by the demands of the job. Delegation isn't simply letting others do jobs for you or the school, it's also enabling others to take on more responsibility and to play a fuller part in the school.

Moreover, delegation should allow you to play a stronger role in the professional life of the school. To fulfil your part in developing the quality of teaching and learning in the school, you will need to delegate. Sometimes you will also need to delegate this task to the deputy and others so that they too can focus on quality. But by being organised, using time efficiently, delegating to others and upping the voltage of colleagues, you should also be enabling yourself to be fully involved in monitoring the curriculum in action and in reviewing the quality of teaching and learning.

Professional development

On being appointed to a headship, you will have reached a high point in your career ambitions. But at the same time, you will be embarking on a new journey of personal discovery and learning. To support you in your new role, you need to consider the three options already discussed on page 7:

- mentoring,
- local support groups,
* professional development via, for example, the HEADLAMP scheme.

Beyond these, you might also consider accredited courses and modules and other opportunities for professional development. Heads certainly need to keep abreast of issues to do with

- school improvement
- effective schools
- effective teaching
- school management and leadership
- pupils' learning
- curriculum areas
- pastoral care
- behaviour management.

Chapter 8 **Managing yourself**

Some heads regard their own professional learning as something which comes after other staff members' needs have been met. Of course, heads need to share out limited staff development funds. However, they are entitled to some of this money and should invest some of it in themselves. Indeed, heads who participate in professional development activities are modelling the importance of life-long learning. If they appear not to need any further professional development why should other members of staff bother?

Professional development, especially off-site activities, also provides heads with much needed time to reflect, opportunities to keep up-to-date and the chance to look beyond their own school and learn about other schools and approaches. Without such enrichment, headship can quickly become a narrow role and heads who don't nourish themselves in these ways can become impoverished.

Personal time

There are always competing priorities for your attention. Furthermore, there is never a time when the work is 'completed'. Headship, like teaching, is an open-ended job. There is always something more to do, or something to do better. That is the excitement of the job – it is varied and challenging. But as was said earlier headship can also be a treadmill.

If there is no end to the work, then the tasks just keep on coming and coming. And some heads respond by keeping on and on, sometimes to the point of exhaustion. Heads may possess long-life batteries, but even these run down and need recharging.

Heads need to be tenacious, dogged and hard-working. But

they also need to be self-disciplined enough to say, 'Tonight, I am having a break. This evening I am doing something else'. In other words, heads need to preserve time for themselves, their families and their friends.

Tired heads don't make effective leaders. Exhausted heads are no good to anybody. So heads need to be self-monitoring and should recognise the signs of strain and try to alleviate some of the pressures when they can. Some heads occasionally work at home for a morning to get 'on top' of the paperwork and to clear the in-tray. Others have a sense of protected time when they normally aim not to do any school work – they go home earlier on a Friday evening or keep Saturdays completely clear. Some ensure they never do more than two nights a week back in school or at least manage their diaries with vigilance and care.

There are many strategies for coping. What's important is that you establish and hold onto the principle of protecting some of your own time.

These three sets of issues – organisation, professional development and personal time – are important strategies for making the workload realistic and the job 'do-able'. In a sense, they are professional, psychological and physical survival strategies. They should help you to cope with the rigours and demands of the work. They should also help you to enjoy the role. One further idea is that at least once a term you reflect on the school's – and your own – successes.

- How do you know you are doing a good job?
- What are the signs of success?
- What is currently going wrong?
- What has improved?

Chapter 8 **Managing yourself**

These are serious questions to ask and to answer. Like everyone else, heads need to feel valued and one way to do this is for you to consider the recent and current areas of progress in the school.

Conclusion

It might be useful to set out some of the key things heads need to try to keep in mind as they go about their work. The following list is by no means exhaustive or exclusive. It simply represents some of the main things heads should strive to do daily as they work in and around the school. The points are not presented in any order of priority.

1 Communicate with colleagues and stakeholders

Keep the channels of communication open. Talk with as many colleagues as possible. Let others hear your concerns, interests, values and ideas.

2 Promote the successes and strengths of the school

Tell people about how well the school is doing. Be seen to recognise the strengths of the school. Value the achievements of pupils and praise them to parents and governors. Recognise the enterprise of staff and value their efforts.

3 Consult and make decisions

Ask colleagues and stakeholders for their ideas and thoughts about developments. Seek a multi-perspective view on specific issues. But do not be afraid to make a decision yourself. When no clear consensus emerges it is for you to decide.

4 Involve the deputy

Strive to develop a professional partnership with the deputy. Use her as a sounding board. Involve her in consultations and communications. Ensure the deputy has a role to play in monitoring the quality of teaching and learning.

5 Focus on teaching and learning

Visit classrooms, talk teaching, observe lessons, teach groups, tour the school looking for patterns and key themes in the classrooms. Look at staff members' teaching plans and evaluations. Encourage staff to talk about pupils' progress. Ask questions and listen to colleagues' answers and responses.

6 Monitor whether the school's aims, plans and policies are being implemented.

Examine whether the school's educational, social and moral values are firmly in place. Check whether the priorities in the school's development plan are being achieved. Are established policies being put into operation, where and to what extent?

7 Ensure that there are clear structures and systems which provide a sense of organisation and efficiency

Internal and external communications should flow smoothly. The school office should function well. School finances should be well managed and check systems built in. Files, orders and stock controls should be in place. Equipment and plant should be in good working order.

8 The chair of governors should be known to all staff

The chairperson should be involved in the school. She should talk to the deputy head as well as other staff. From time to time, she should visit the school during the working day.

9 The head should have an overview of the school

The head should know what is going on in the school. She should be 'connected' and 'plugged-in' to internal issues and debates in the school. She should also be aware of the governors' concerns and of those of parents and other stakeholders. The head should listen and treat seriously the views of others, even when they differ from or challenge her own.

10 The head should try to establish and sustain a sense of whole school

The head should appreciate the work of groups and teams in the school. The head should try to develop consistency of approach amongst staff. The head needs to try to unite staff in a spirit of working together and of sharing professional concerns and developments.

Further reading

Bolam, R, McMahon, A, Pocklington, K and **Weindling, D** (1993) *Effective Management in Schools*. London: DFE.

Fullan, M (1991) *The New Meaning of Educational Change*. London: Cassell.

Fullan, M and **Hargreaves, A** (1992) *What's Worth Fighting for in your School?* Buckingham: Open University Press.

Mortimore, P, Sammons, P, Stoll, L, Lewis, D and **Ecob, R** (1988) *School Matters*. Wells: Open Books.

Nias, J (1987) One finger, one thumb: A case study of the deputy head's part in the of a nursery and infant school in **Southworth, G** (ed.) *Readings in Primary School Management*. London: Falmer Press

Nias, J, Southworth, G and **Yeomans, R** (1989) *Staff Relationships in the Primary School*. London: Cassell.

Skelton, M (1991) Time management in *Primary File*, files 12 and 13.

Southworth, G (1994) Two heads are better than one, in *Managing Schools Today*, November/December issue.

Southworth, G (1995) It takes two to tango: Characteristics of successful head and deputy partnerships, in *Managing Schools Today*, September issue.

Southworth, G (1995) *Talking Heads: Voices of Experience – An investigation into Primary Headship in the 1990s*. Cambridge: University of Cambridge Institute of Education.

Index

Consultation 9, 21, 22, 56, 69
Culture 21, 31-32, 52, 55
Curriculum 3, 10, 29, 33, 45, 49, 54, 56, 64

Delegation 63
Deputy head 9, 38-39, 70

Governor 2, 4, 9, 17, 59, 70

Leadership 2, 4, 12, 16, 20-23, 25-36, 42, 44, 64

Monitoring 13, 28

Organisation 1, 3, 16, 23, 34, 48, 62, 66

Parents 4, 5, 9, 16-18, 33, 34, 59
Policies 2, 3, 11-12, 13, 15, 39, 46, 51, 69

Professional development 9, 15, 20, 62, 64-66
Pupils 4, 20, 28, 38, 50
Teachers 15, 22, 31, 47-49, 51-52, 56-57
Time management 63

Also available from **primary** file publishing

Each **Primary File Guide** deals with an issue of current and lasting concern to teachers. Thoroughly researched and written in a clear, concise style, the series includes the following titles.

The Primary File Guide to... Dealing with Medical Matters in School

Dr Martin Blackwell

Every day in school a child is sick or hurt and requires quick and effective medical attention. Written by a practising GP, this handy guide provides immediately accessible, practical advice on recognising and dealing with illness, infection and injury in the classroom and the playground.

isbn 1 874050 16 3

The Primary File Guide to... Surviving as an NQT

Julie Jennings

Being an NQT can be a trying and demanding experience. The pressures of a new job, combined with the everyday demands of the classroom, can be highly stressful. Julie Jennings provides the practical support every newly-qualified teacher needs. Written from personal experience, this guide will help you get through your first year of teaching with a little more confidence. It is also a valuable resource for experienced mentors and other teachers working alongside NQTs.

isbn 1 874050 27 9

Also available from pfp

The Primary File Guide to... Deputy Headship
Lynn Cousins

The role of the deputy head has changed and developed over the years. The deputy head is now expected to take on many of the responsibilities of running a primary school at the same time as managing a class and often performing other specific duties. This book looks at the need for deputy heads and at what is required to succeed in the position. It looks closely at the qualities you need to be an effective deputy head and at how you can develop in the role. If you also see the position of deputy as a training for headship then there is advice on how to use the opportunities for advancement to the full.

isbn 1 874050 29 5

The Primary File Guide to... Assessment
Colin Connor

As the debate about accountability and added value gather momentum, the issue of assessment will be focussed on more than ever. The inevitable conflict between the educational and political uses of assessment means that every teacher needs a clear understanding of the issues, both to guide their own classroom and school practice and to respond to publicly raised issues. This succinct guide sums up these issues clearly and concisely. All of the major issues are included – ways of assessing, recording assessments, observation, moderation and more. The book concludes with an up-to-date analysis of the 1995 assessment requirements.

isbn 1 874050 18 X

Also available from pfp

The Primary File Guide to... Producing School Policies

Martin Skelton and David Playfoot

Policies are a vital part of creating an effective school, but there is little real help on how to produce and implement policies that actually work. This practical book provides the answer by covering all the key issues: What is a policy? Why does it matter? How to produce a policy. How to put it into practice. How to review and maintain its effectiveness.

isbn 1 874050 13 9

The Primary File Guide to... Effective Teaching

Martin Skelton and David Playfoot

Of all the factors which lead to children learning effectively, the way we teach in the classroom is one over which we have a reasonable degree of control. So knowing something about teaching effectively is important for every teacher. Over the past few years, our understanding of the issues behind effective teaching has grown – this book summarises simply and accessibly what we now know. Each chapter covers a key aspect of teaching, including teaching styles, planning, assessment, recording and reporting, relationships and more. Written with the practitioner in mind, it will help individual teachers and whole staffs to further their understanding of this important issue.

isbn 1 874050 22 8

Also available from pfp

The Primary File Guide to... Reporting to Parents

Graham Reeves

Every primary teacher accepts the importance of reporting to parents. The legislation demands that parents are reported to; more importantly the link between school and home is understood to be an important part of helping children to progress and develop as they move through the school; and the way parents are reported to does much to build (or lose) their confidence in their child's school. This book provides a clear and accessible guide to the main issues and is written to provide practical help to teachers and schools. Chapters include: How to report to parents; What parents should know; Reporting formats; How to write reports, and Parents' evenings.

isbn 1 874050 21 X

The Primary File Guide to... School Development Plans

Martin Skelton and David Playfoot

School development plans are now an everyday part of running a school. They help to ensure that real progress is made and that staff, the management team, governors and OFSTED-trained inspectors are all aware of the priorities and plans. This guide identifies what school development plans really are and what they can do for your school. It gives the six key areas for planning and discusses the writing of targets and the identification of success criteria and priorities. This is, essentially, a practical guide and so shows you how to make the most of development plans in your school.

isbn 1 874050 24 4

format – 64-80 pages, 130mm x 197mm